# NEW SKIN

## HEATHER WALTERS

First paperback edition 2022

*Book design and cover by Natalia Junqueira*
*Editing by Joie Davidow*

Hardback ISBN 979-8-9872371-0-6
Paperback ISBN 979-8-9872371-1-3
Ebook ISBN 979-8-9872371-2-0

*Dedicated first and foremost to God who guided me through every part of this book, my two boys Conner and Cameron, my sister and my mother who also survived.*

*To my friends who have supported me through this journey and to all the strangers that I have met on the road who have impacted who I am today!*

*Thank you for the people who came into my life for a season that have inspired me to tell my story!*

# Contents

# Preface

Did you know that every seven to ten years we shed our skins and
our bodies renew themselves?
Can we heal ourselves with our mindsets?
Does holistic medicine work?
Why did people start using Reiki and sound therapy to heal various
diseases?

I never knew my purpose in this world. I lived in a religious com-
munity and battled cancer twice, so I've done a lot of healing. When
you're broken at a young age, you wonder if you can put yourself back
together. You can. And in this book, I'll share the story of a broken
girl who went through many trials and tribulations and learned not
only to love herself but to cure herself.

Self-love has been one of the most important aspects of my life,
loving myself through pain and suffering has been the greatest gift I've
given myself. I've learned that forgiving others is the key to peace and
happiness. I've used extensive therapy, self-help books, spiritual healing,
Reiki and many other methods to improve my health and wellbeing.

Now I've written this book to help other women prosper and
become strong, courageous, confident and independent. Having
complete trust and confidence in a higher power has brought me

through the most troublesome times in my life. A vision of whom I wanted to become gave me the strength to continue to push forward and make my dreams a reality.

What are your strengths?
What do you dream of becoming?
What are you willing to sacrifice to reach your goals?
Through the years I've had to ask myself all these questions in order to become the woman I am today.

Faith, meaning complete trust and confidence in something or someone, helps us grow through moments that might tear us down. Determination means pushing forward through obstacles that might block us from attaining our goals. Anyone who tries to accomplish something will be met with roadblocks, but strength and faith will get them through.

"Knowing yourself is the beginning of all wisdom"

Aristotle

# Chapter 1
# IMAGINATION LEADS TO MOTIVATION

I have the power to be whoever I want to be! I always loved to daydream and think about whom I'd become when I got older. I'd sit in my room writing about random things as my mind wandered into the deep abyss of thought. Sometimes it made sense to me. Sometimes it made no sense at all. I often wondered why some people from broken families were successful, while others kept repeating the same toxic cycle. Why did some people reach their goals while others were never able to get to that point? Are some people more motivated than others? Fear was always the root cause when I failed to accomplish my dreams, and it's the same for others.

I had a vision of my future. I wanted to do something in life that would outlive me. I wanted a legacy to live on after I left this world. The way to get motivated to do anything in life is to discipline yourself to take that first step. Fear stops most of us. I had to change that within myself, and I knew that once I did, I'd find freedom.

I don't come from an educated family, but I didn't want that to stop me. I've read stories of homeless people who lived in their cars for years but were determined to become whatever they dreamt of being. Your upbringing doesn't have to limit who you become. Mindset and determination can take you anywhere.

It about getting out of your routine, changing something in your life every day. Your circumstances don't define your destina-

1

tion. Believe in yourself. Get motivated. Find someone you can look up to and create that vision for yourself.

Whenever I really work on myself and see myself prospering, I realize I've outgrown the person I was. Life is a constant process of growing and changing. We take a leap forward and then there's another step and another. It appears we never reach the end. The more we learn, the less we know.

T.S. Elliott said, "Only those who will risk going too far can possibly find out how far one can go."

If you want to make changes in your life, you have to take chances. I wanted to be the one person in my family who managed to change course. I took many risks—some turned out well, others did not. Several times when I took a leap of faith, I was surprised that it opened more doors for me.

Life is about preparing for the future. If you're working towards something, what is your purpose? If you have no purpose in life, you're left with loneliness and emptiness.

Many successful people have failed numerous times before finally getting a big breakthrough. Thomas Edison failed more than a thousand times in his struggle to invent the light bulb. He had determination. James Dyson failed to invent the vacuum cleaner more than five thousand times before he finally got a patent that now is worth over three billion dollars. Success doesn't come from giving up.

The problem is that we want to be successful, but fear stops us. We reach a plateau and life stops. Most people are happy when they reach that plateau. Very few of us seek more, but those who do have a vision, determination and drive.

Neuroscientists have found that the brain activity of those who listen to motivational speeches or even feel-good music shows that they are inspired. Uplifting music triggers dopamine in the brain. So does a fun outing, a date or any feel-good moment. Our brains don't know the difference between what's really happening and what we think about. We can get the same rise in dopamine level by envisioning positive things as we do when they really happen.

Which explains the placebo effect. Studies show that forty percent of patients who are given a placebo and told it will make them better actually improve. Our thoughts are capable of manifesting reality.

The first time I was diagnosed with cancer, a high school friend told me, "Cancer is 10% disease and 90% attitude." I wasn't sure how I felt about that when she said it, but I tried using it. I researched how the mind works and found studies measuring brain activity by thought alone.

In ancient Greece, sound was used to treat mental illness. In the nineteenth century, doctors found a connection between sound and healing, and discovered that music actually increased the flow of blood.

Throughout my battle with cancer, whenever I had surgery, the doctors played music for me. It gave me a sense of calmness. I've always turned to music when I've felt sad or hurt.

I'd hike in the woods listening to classical music and get lost in my thoughts. It gives me a serene feeling. At times, I've gone for a drive in my car with no destination in mind, the sunroof open and the music turned up so loud I felt free and alive, because I was living in the moment, savoring every turn and curve as I drove up the coastline. I wasn't waiting on anyone to give me permission to live like this. I was in a state of joy!

Did the music give me that feeling of contentment? Could I manifest it simply by playing uplifting music? It seemed to work quite well. I made a playlist on my phone of music that inspired me—anything from classical music to hip hop to classic rock. Whenever I started to feel a little sad, I'd turn on that playlist and it made me feel happy again. I could summon that contented feeling just by listening to my playlist.

I also found inspiration in reading books and motivational speakers. Reading improves your memory and concentration. It helps to reduce stress levels and provides enjoyment. Stimulating the brain, can alleviate numerous ailments.

My determination to survive cancer was a huge inspiration to the people around me. I tried traditional treatments like chemotherapy and radiation. I read a lot of books and joined cancer support groups that practiced holistic medicine. I got in touch with a couple of people in other countries who guided me to helpful, natural remedies.

The problem with chemotherapy is that it only works temporarily. At times, its needed to blast the cancer cells to prevent them from metastasizing. But the side effects are beyond anything you can imagine if you haven't experienced it.

The people I met in the support group told me how antiparasitic drugs helped fight cancer. The causes of cancer range from what we eat, to the way we exercise, environmental issues and so forth. Studies have shown that genetics play a very small role.

I was tested for eighty-eight different genes and was negative for all of them. Studies now show that obesity plays a big role, which goes hand and hand with the foods we eat.

My motivation to stay alive led me to investigate alternative treatments. Four years ago, I was given six months to live. When I first battled cancer, I went vegan for a couple years. Then I slowly incorporated meat into my diet and my cancer came back. I went back to a vegan diet and ate lots of vegetables. I started taking daily supplements, from raw apricot seeds to apple cider vinegar and various mushroom extracts, to FDA-approved medicines my oncologist recommended. I also did a lot of juicing and making smoothies. It was a way to get in all my nutrition without having to eat foods I dislike.

Scientists have found that the number one factor in almost every disease is stress. Stress causes high blood pressure, heart problems, anxiety, fertility problems, and many other diseases. It weakens the immune system, allowing diseases to flourish. I began eliminating stress in my life. I practiced yoga and meditation. I started exercising again. I took people out of my life who caused stress. And if I couldn't avoid them, I learned to express my feelings in tactful ways that didn't sound condescending.

My Hispanic mother never sugar coated anything. I didn't grow up with tactful people, so I had to learn it. As I started traveling for work, I encountered situations in which I wasn't very tactful and hurt people's feelings. A woman who worked with me told me I needed to watch what I said and the way I said it. I made it a mission to start working on that. I've always been very receptive when people point out things I need to improve. I want to continue to improve myself and help others.

I met a woman in Washington DC who told me that coming to the United States to attend medical school had been very challenging to her. She explained that she'd needed a lot of patience. She couldn't speak proper English, which made every aspect of her life difficult. When she was pulled over for speeding, she couldn't understand the officer, which made for a very difficult situation. She thought the officer was going to kill her and became terribly afraid. She'd gotten out of her car to approach the officer not understanding why he was so upset with her. The story was a bit comical.

People who come to the States from abroad inspire me because in order to make such a journey, they must have a vision and the determination to make it a reality.

In Ohio, I worked with a Ukrainian woman, and we became friends and then roommates. She had been awarded an athletic scholarship to a university in the United States and become very successful. When I asked her how she felt leaving her mother to pursue her studies here, she explained that her mother encouraged her.

I loved traveling because it gave me so many opportunities to meet people from all walks of life, religions, and ethnicities. I have always been open to learning about them and about myself and they have taught me so much. Meeting a wide variety of people has motivated me to become a better person, to eat healthier foods, and to outgrow the old me. I learned about many different supplements and healthy foods.

Another thing that has inspired me to push forward is my faith in God. Sometimes when we find ourselves in uncomfortable situations, we think we are being punished for our sins or being attacked for some evil we've committed, but in reality, God wants us to go through hard times for our own development. We are called to go through difficulties in order to strengthen us. What you walk through determines what you walk in. It can be impossible to understand life until we experience it for ourselves.

If we give up when the going gets tough, we lose. Every situation prepares us for something bigger, whether it's another lesson or getting to the next place in our lives. If God gave us everything we ever wanted, we would self-destruct. We must be thankful for the hard times in life. That was the nature of the cross. If we dodge difficult situations, we become weak.

Resistance is good. A shift in morality is the fruit of intimacy with our Lord Father. The more garbage you put in your life, the more garbage you put out. That is why negativity in any aspect of life is bad, whether it's watching the news, listening to gossip, and even being around negative people. If we keep those things in our lives, they program us to think negatively.

Every day when I went for chemotherapy, I arrived smiling and happy, but as I looked around at everyone else fighting the same battle, I saw that they were sad and worn out. Chemo makes you feel tired and weak. I saw that the other patients looked at me judgmentally. But happiness is very contagious.

One of my friends told me," Every time I had dark days in my life, I stopped to think about you and the way you kept pushing forward, and I'd think I could go on, because you did. She started crying as she told me. It was a very heartfelt moment. When people tell me stories like this, it inspires me and motivates me to continue even on the darkest of days. When I was fighting cancer, if I had given up, I would have lost everything. God was taking me through that trial to help me become stronger and to lead me where I was meant to be.

Many times, I've I had to tell myself words of affirmation to get through hardship. After a while, I began to believe the words I told myself:

I am strong.

I can do this.

God didn't bring me this far to give up!

It gave me a sense of self-worth and motivated me. It challenged me to get to the next level with cancer, and that inspired me.

Throughout life, any obstacle or tragedy I've encountered has inspired me to get through it. When I look back, I see how far I've come and where I'm going. I've had the ambition to get through whatever I've faced, and I've been eager to accomplish things. Seeing the way people achieve a lot by pushing forward has inspired me.

The love and support of my family, parents, church, friends and even strangers has inspired me. The numerous cards, letters and gifts I received while battling cancer motivated me. I love the saying, "Every day is a chance to be better." Your mind can take you to your goals. All the money in the world can't buy your health. Gratitude is the assurance of health. So, appreciate everything you may be going through and know that it is bringing you to a better place.

# Chapter 2
# RELIGIOUS CULT

Cancer will cause my emotional collapse today. My doctor just got my MRI results, and the cancer is still there, although he said the results are a bit ambiguous, so they'll rescan in another month.

I was in remission for a year, then the dreadful cancer migrated with a vengeance. I saw a doctor who treats cancer from a molecular level and changes its genetic sequencing. I'm living day by day. At the age of forty-four, I have begun to ponder my life before cancer. I was diagnosed at thirty-nine, a young- verging-on-middle-aged woman, traveling the world, making great money, hitting the bars, meeting new people, enjoying my life. I'd fly across the country for a weekend.

I've always said I've lived a compelling life, and I thought the fun would never end. Then I was forced to realize that death could come knocking on my door, and my life, the world I knew, could end abruptly.

This is the story of the psychopath who haunted my family for years and damaged us beyond anything conceivable. I survived, but several of my siblings did not. It all started in a small town on the gulf coast of Florida

I was born into a chaotic world. My mother and father were so happy, they exuded joy and were elated to welcome a new addition to the family. Well, that's not exactly how it began. I'm not sure about the happiness, but the psychopath was happy to have another innocent child to abuse. My father was an American Indian with the temper of a roaring beast. I don't know much about his upbringing, but his mother had been married several times and he had five sisters. Before he married my mother, he was a Seabee in the Navy.

I've heard many stories about his life. This one comes to mind: When he was fourteen years old, his mother told him to put on his best clothes because he had a big day at school. She took him to the bus stop, and he didn't see her again until he was an adult. I don't know what happened during those years, but I'm sure some of it was horrible. My father hated women. He abused everyone in his life, whether it was the women he married or his own kids.

My mother was Cuban, born and raised in an area of Miami called "Little Cuba" because of the ethnicity there. She was a typical Cuban lady, Spanish-speaking, strong willed, hardheaded, and beautiful.

She was Catholic, raised primarily by her mother. Her dad had been married numerous times. He loved women and I believe he cheated on most of those he was involved with. Later in life, my mother had a relationship with her father but early on, he was not around.

My grandmother was quite pragmatic, and I loved her so much. She was very independent and growing up, I was compared to her because of my love of travel. After she divorced my grandfather, she never remarried. She traveled as long as she could. Her favorite country was Portugal. I haven't been there yet, but I plan on it.

My mother gave me a newspaper article from the sixties that reported my grandfather was running for the Cuban senate. Perhaps that's where I get my desire to keep pushing forward in life, and to be the person God created me to be. When she was very young, my mother's father left the family, and that had an impact on her perception of what a husband and father should be. Unfortunately, as a child we imitate what we see. We tend to forget the good times and remember the bad ones. My own childhood was diminished by the traumatic events in our home.

10

My parents met in Miami. My mom was working at a local grocery store and my dad was persistent. Apparently, he won that battle. My mother was very religious, so she waited to consummate her marriage. It must have been a huge shock when she discovered she'd married a pedophile. Her marriage was not a white picket fence and a loving family and happily ever after. It was a horror story. One pregnancy after another—two boys and two girls.

Fast forward and I was the youngest. I remember sitting on the couch with my siblings listening to my dad beat the hell out of our mother in the bedroom as she screamed and begged him to stop. We couldn't help her. We were all under the age of ten, so young we couldn't do anything but listen, holding each other in fear. He'd come out of the bedroom like nothing had happened, but we could hear our mother crying.

My dad told my brothers things like, "take my boots off," and if they didn't do it fast enough for him, he'd kick them in the face with steal toed boots. They were kids, innocent little children. Once, my brother found a rabbit he wanted to keep as a pet. The next day my dad killed the rabbit, cooked it and fed it to us for dinner. After we ate it, he told us it was my brother's rabbit.

He was such a cruel human being. I was so young, I'm not sure what my brother did, but I'm sure he was sad that we ate his pet for dinner. Abuse makes you cold to people. It can make you emotionless. The people who should have been my role models were hurting me. My parents were supposed to show me love and kindness and teach me to ride a bike, to read me bedtime stories. I never remember anything like that.

I experienced things no child should ever experience. My father kept chickens, and he made us all break their necks to kill them. We didn't dare refuse anything he told us to do. I don't know what would have happened if we'd stood up to him, but we were all too scared to find out.

11

Another time, my neighbor's dog was hanging around our house. My brother Josh was always a mischievous little boy. He picked me up and put me on the dog's back and told me it was a horse. I pulled the dog by his ears, and he bit my face. I was rushed to the hospital and left with thirteen stiches. Later that evening when my father got home, he took his rifle and shot the dog. He was the evilest human being I have ever encountered.

Every Sunday we were in church confessing all the wrong he was doing. According to my father, God forgave him because he repented his sins. Really? How was that possible? How could my father be a pedophile, abuse my mother, kill animals like it was nothing without any remorse at all? Would God really forgive him? How could God, who loves me, allow me to experience such pain and suffering? I was an innocent child.

As an adult, I realized that God could redeem any situation and bring benefits into your life as a result of the suffering. Listening to my father abuse my mother, then hearing him talk about God was confusing. Every Sunday, we sat in the pews of one church or another. It didn't matter the denomination. If we confessed our sins and promised to be a better person, God would forgive us no matter what.

Religion was a primary focus in our home. At night before bed, we all had to kneel beside the bed and pray for forgiveness. What the heck were we praying for? At the age of three or four surely, I had not been that bad.

My father continued to abuse my mother, and when he felt he had total control over her, he started on us. He controlled us by torturing us until he destroyed us. He abused us physically, emotionally, psychologically, and sexually, including my brothers whom he beat almost to death, and if they cried, he'd say, "Take it like a man!" They were innocent children.

I couldn't understand why my father was so mean. He had so much anger. Growing up in this deranged family, I thought no one would ever be able relate to me. We were very poor, and my dad was always hustling to make money. He wouldn't allow my mother to work. My grandmother sent us boxes of food so we'd have something to eat.

In 1984 after fifteen years of marriage, my mother left my father. What made me the saddest was that my two brothers went to Florida with my dad and my sister and I stayed with our mother in North Carolina. The only time I'd had with my brothers had been traumatic. I still have questions about why they were sent away with my father. They endured his abuse until they were eighteen. As time passed, it felt like they didn't exist anymore.

My mom was busy trying to support us, so she was never home. My older sister became like a mother to me. She really took care of me, but I was the little sister who had to keep all the secrets from mom. She was into boys and sometimes she'd sneak out of the house, threatening me like any other sibling, but I kept her secrets safe. I needed her. Mom and my sister didn't get along. There are multiple reasons why. Mainly, it was the blame game. I always tried to stay neutral because I loved them both.

Three years after my parents split up, my mom began dating a man who seemed nice, although we didn't think much about him. He was just Mom's boyfriend. I think he tried to be a father figure to us, but my sister and I were already broken. Two years later, when I was twelve, this man became my stepfather.

My sister went back to Florida, and I was alone, being raised by this new man and my mom. I was very sad. All my siblings were gone. I was starting a new school and this should have been my time to shine. I wanted to forget the past and start over again. I always imagined I could be whoever I wanted to me. I was determined to create a new image for myself, a beautiful little girl with a loving mother and father. The typical American family.

And I did. At my new school, I made friends quickly, but I never allowed myself to get close to anyone. How could I? What if they found out who I really was or where I came from? Could I ever fit in with the kids my age? After all the turmoil I had lived through, I wanted a normal life like the other kids.

I went to church regularly and there I met my best friend and confidant. She knew a lot about me but not everything. Sometimes we'd skip church on Wednesdays and go joy riding around town. We did innocent things, just two teenagers trying to have a little fun. I wondered if the people at church were like my father behind closed doors, and I wanted to know what my role was in all this brokenness.

# Chapter 3
# CALLOW

I had to grow out of my fears and into my accomplishments. My stepfather was an intelligent, hardworking man. He had what everyone yearns for—loving parents who had been married for sixty years. The family you read about in fairytales. Our new family had cookouts and invited friends and relatives to the house. It was nice. I had never known this kind of life before.

I felt I was a part of something bigger, but I was still alone because all my siblings were gone. I told myself that maybe, just maybe, if I could push my previous life out of my mind and enjoy this moment, it would all go away. It worked for a while, but when you're broken, you're broken, and no matter how hard you try, you can't push the pain away. The abuse had damaged my perception of the world, and set me up to self-destruct.

When I was fifteen, I ran away from home. My parents were very strict, and I detested their rules. I went to the home of distant family members who were in their twenties. They got me drunk and tried to have sex with me, but I forced them away and took off running. My parents called the cops, and that night, I was picked up and taken to juvenile hall.

It was like jail. I had to strip off my clothes in front of a female guard who made me put on a pair of dark blue pants and a light blue shirt. Then she put all my belongings in a bag and took me to what looked like a cell with a narrow bed, a toilet and a little square window on the door. I was the only girl there, and the boys really liked that. I was not allowed to talk to the opposite sex, and since there were no other girls, I couldn't talk to anyone. The guards let us out to watch television in the commons area and have snacks, but at bedtime, we were locked up.

It was supposed to teach me a lesson. The only thing it taught me was that getting in trouble wasn't that bad. Juvenile Hall was just a bunch of kids rebelling against their parents. They were all broken, like me. Twenty-four hours later, the cops took me to a courthouse where I had to give my word of honor to stay out of trouble until I was sixteen, which was only a few months away.

I don't remember having a significant birthday. It was just a normal day, but to me, it was the day when my parents couldn't control me anymore. I left home to go to a party, got drunk again, and two guys in their twenties tried to rape me. I kept kicking them off, but they kept grabbing me and holding me down. Someone across the hall heard me. He opened his bedroom door and said, "Come in here." I looked at him with fear in my eyes. He said, "I'm not going to hurt you. "I slept in his bed while he watched over me. He saved me that night and I will be forever grateful. The next morning, my arms and legs were covered in bruises.

At the age of seventeen, I was introduced to heavy drugs, and I soon overdosed. I was at a friend's house, sitting on the bathroom floor vomiting a white substance. For a moment, I thought this is the end of my life. My friends were slapping my face saying," Stay with me girl, come on, stay with me!" That's the last thing I remember of that night.

I survived but it didn't stop there. I'd cut lines on a box of cigarettes in nightclub bathrooms. It gave me a feeling of euphoria and I'd dance until the early hours. For once, I felt no pain. I didn't feel worthless. I was indispensable. I could dance the night away, confident and excited.

When the drugs wore off, I felt worthless again. I tried to get away from it, but when you're in that lifestyle it's all around you. Sometimes when I was by myself, I'd write my feelings down or write poetry. During that time, I wrote this poem:

### CALLOW

Burning fire in a field
Stars light in the sky
Will I ever get to say Goodbye?
Triumphant but discouraged
Despairingly wondering
Will it change before my eyes?
Or is it just lies
Trapped in my mind?
Is it all just a sign?
Time will resume
As if all imagined.

This poem expressed my life perfectly. Was I imagining this life? I wanted something different, and I could stay clean for a while. Then I'd meet up with the same crowd and there I was cutting lines in a night club bathroom. A couple of people I knew from the party scene had died of overdoses, and I knew If I didn't stop I'd be next. Sometimes I was homeless. I'd wheedle up enough money to stay in a hotel or crash at a friend's house. Sometime between the ages of seventeen and eighteen, I submitted a long poem to a poetry contest and won the state prize.

At the age of eighteen, I cleaned up my life and stayed away from those toxic people. I started working at a textile factory where you could make good money straight out of high school. I bought my first car, rented my own apartment and lived by myself. It was comforting. I met a guy who became my husband. He was an air traffic controller in the Marines. Our relationship was toxic, but that's all

I'd ever known. The abuse was mostly verbal, sometimes physical. He was about four years older, and I was so broken, I had no idea what a healthy relationship looked like.

I was determined to make something of myself. I wanted to go to college, to become someone better than my parents had been. Neither of them had gotten further than a high school diploma. I wanted to work in the medical field. I always felt a presence, as if someone was watching over me. I just knew there was so much more out there in this world.

My boyfriend/ husband was very supportive. But we said horrible things to one another. I was damaged, beyond reparable, or so I thought. I had deep insecurities, feelings of worthlessness, abandonment issues and the list goes on and on. I got pregnant. Marriage and a beautiful child were what I wanted. I wanted that perfect little family. I wanted a husband who would love me like I had never been loved before. I wanted a child who would love me endlessly and I could protect from all the evil people like my father. I wanted a home and a beautiful yard. My husband made sure I had that. I envisioned my child playing on a hot sunny day sliding on the slide or swinging from the tire hanging in the tree while mommy planted her garden.

Then my stepfather came to our house while my husband was out, and my life came crashing down. He said "Your mother and I are going to take you to have an abortion. You're too young to have a child. You have your whole life ahead of you." I was crying. I was torn. I had a decision to make because during this time, I had gotten an offer to be one of the Hawaiian Tropic Models, living in California or Hawaii. The broken little girl had landed a modeling gig. It was the dream of a lifetime, but I was pregnant.

When my husband came home, I cried and told him what my stepfather said. This story ends with a handsome little blonde, blue eyed boy who is my entire life. Having a child at the age of twenty-one was challenging. I was going to college, being a mother and a wife, and trying to figure out who I was.

I hadn't acknowledged the healing I needed to do, and because I was a broken parent, I was only going down the same road my parents had taken. At three in the morning, on January 23rd, 1998, my sister called. She said, "Our brother Gary is in critical condition in the hospital. We don't know the details yet, but it's bad!"

I hung up and told my husband we had to go to Florida. When we arrived at the hospital, Gary was unconscious. All we knew was that somebody had thrown him from a car outside the emergency department and taken off. The surveillance cameras had caught it.

My brother had a head trauma, as if someone had struck him with an object. He didn't make it. He was murdered at the age of twenty-four. I hadn't experienced death before. He was gone, and was never coming back. Our last conversation hadn't been pleasant. I'd confronted him about what he'd done to me when I was nine. He'd taken something from me I could never get back. I didn't get to tell him I forgave him for stealing part of my childhood, my self-esteem, and my ability to trust men.

We prepared for the funeral. My mother, sister, and I stood over the casket and cried our eyes out. It seemed surreal. His body was stiff, his eyes closed. It didn't even look like him. The trauma on his head was hidden under a baseball cap. He never wore a baseball cap! He always put gel in his hair. It seemed as if any minute he'd open his eyes and tell me it was all a joke.

That moment changed me forever. The abuse was over and I forgave him. That door was closed. Unfortunately, the marriage ended, and I became a single parent. I never found out what a healthy marriage looked like. Relationship after relationship, abuse after abuse, another child was born, and the cycle continued. The next guy was controlling and jealous and abusive. That's all I'd ever known. I'd been programmed to attract abusive men.

21

I'd seen my father abuse my mother and they loved each other, right? I tried to hide the abuse from my kids, but they saw it just as I had as a child. At times, my son tried to protect me. I thought it was me and my kids against the world, and I would do anything to protect them. I'd take the abuse, because I was the adult, and I could handle it, but no one was ever going to hurt my boys.

It was extremely hard. I worked a full-time job while doing my clinical rotations at school. For a year I worked seventy-two hours a week and did the best I could for my kids. Luckily, I had a good friend who helped me a lot, and I got scholarships to help pay my college tuition. I managed to maintain good grades in college while trying to take care of my children and work. I joke with my oldest son that he pretty much grew up in the hospital, because between work and school he was always with me.

My life was getting better. I was away from drugs, but drinking began. I'd wake up in the morning and guzzle a few beers. What was I doing to myself? When you're broken at a young age, it doesn't go away. I didn't realize that I was packing away more and more hurt. For some reason, I felt I deserved it, that in some way, I was instigating the abuse. At times I even thought if they didn't abuse me, they didn't love me. That's how your mind operates when you come from an abusive family.

My college years were exciting, even as a single parent. I had a little convertible with numerous issues and at times it overheated and stalled. One day I was parked outside a store with my son, waiting for the car to cool down, when I watched a man go into the store. When he came out, he came up to my window and said, "I noticed you're still sitting here, are you waiting on me?" I said, "Oh no, my car overheats. I am just waiting on it to cool down, but I like your shirt." He had some rocker shirt on. We exchanged numbers and chatted a few times. He was a roadie for big performers. One night,

CHAPTER 3

he asked me if I'd like to be backstage while he set up for Rod Stewart. I was like, heck ya! Backstage, I met Rod Stewart's bus roadies. It was awesome. A British guy came up and gave me a rose. I lost touch with that guy, but that's a memory I'll never forget.

We all live in a shell, and maybe if we could step out of it for a moment, we could see what we're capable of.

# Chapter 4
# THE MONSTERS INSIDE HIS HEAD

In 2009, I'd been in a very abusive relationship for about five years, I got an opportunity to move to Savannah, Georgia with my kids and get away from that situation. I was so depressed, I contemplated suicide. I won't go into great detail, because I need to protect my kids.

So, I started a new life in another state. It was challenging, because I got judged a lot. I started working at a local hospital and made new friends. It was another chance to create my own identity. Savannah was a fun place. There were plenty of bars and the beach was nearby.

I met some memorable people, one of whom made a huge impact on who I am today. I began dating a tall, handsome, Italian police officer with a beautiful smile. He was one of the best-looking men I'd ever seen, and I was smitten. He was a fun guy. We'd go out to the bars and drink together. Sometimes, he'd flirt with the women to get us free drinks, and I'd do the same with the guys. We both enjoyed music, so we always came out to hear the local bands. He was very good to my boys, and I loved his little son. We didn't see his daughters much, but they were two of the most beautiful girls I'd ever seen. He had two ex-wives, both beautiful, as well.

I couldn't believe that I'd caught this guy, and he was all mine. It was too good to be true. I was thirty years old, and he was forty-five.

Yes, he was a lot older, but he was so engaging. He loved beautiful women, so he definitely had a wandering eye. He said, "Breasts are like art. It doesn't matter who they belong to, they're beautiful!" I thought it was funny at the time, and who could argue that women are beautiful people?

His father was a surgeon, and his mother was a nurse. He told me that she'd battled mental illnesses. Sometimes, when he talked about her, he'd get a little teary eyed and go quiet. She'd passed away about six years before I met him. I think his parents' relationship had been unstable at times, but when she was close to death, they'd made amends. His parents divorced long before she passed, and his father remarried and seemed happy in his second marriage.

We saw each other quite a bit. Honestly, we were almost inseparable. When we weren't working, we were together. One night we went out drinking and partying. We both drank beyond our limits. When we came back to my house, we got into an argument. I don't even remember what it was about, but I'm pretty sure it was something trivial. Suddenly, it was like a switch flipped and he started punching me. He beat me so badly, my arms and legs were covered in bruises. I cried myself to sleep that night. He said he loved me. That's what my dad did to my mom when they were married. Did he really love me? Did I just get physical assaulted by this man whom I loved so much?

Have you ever been in a relationship where your partner hit you?
How did that make you feel?
Did you feel you deserved it?
Did deserve it?

The next morning, I told him, "I want you to leave and never come back."

He said, "I'm sorry, and I love you. I promise I'll never do it again!"

26

I wanted so badly to believe him. I loved him so much. I said, "No, I love you, but you have to leave. You will never do that to me again!"

He walked out of my house, and I felt so sad. Why did I want this man after he beat me up? I couldn't understand why I felt the way I did. Was I emulating what I'd seen as a child? In a weird way, I felt as if it was somehow my fault. Did I instigate the argument causing him to lash out at me? I sat in silence for a while, trying to sort out my feelings. I felt so alone, damaged, sad, heartbroken. The dreams I'd entwined with this man were gone.

He texted me and kept apologizing for his behavior, swearing it would never happen again. I wanted to believe him. I wanted to think that since we were both inebriated, it was a one-time ordeal, so I took him back. I loved him so much, I yearned for him whenever I wasn't with him. Our relationship was back to normal. We'd take weekend getaways to Florida, go on dinner cruises. I was so in love with this man. We moved into a glamorous apartment in a gated complex on the upscale side of town with all the amenities—an infinity pool, gym, walking track, dog park.

One day, the past came back to haunt me. He left me at home and went to a local bar owned by a fellow police officer. A lot of the guys from his job went there to hang out. It was a Saturday, and I guess he decided to hang with the guys without telling me. I called him numerous times, but he didn't answer his phone. The longer he stayed away, the madder I got. I didn't understand why he liked to get a rise out of me, or why I allowed him to. It got late, and I decided I'd give him some of his own medicine. I went to a bar and got hammered.

When he finally decided to come home, I was still out. I've always been pretty attractive, so guys were hitting on me. When he called me, I ignored him. It was my turn now. I was having fun, chatting with guys, totally innocent. Intoxication makes you lose your cognitive skills. I was starting to feel more confident and chattier. My inhibitions were low, my reaction time to his calls obliterated. I was so intoxicated I couldn't drive home, so I left my car at the bar, which was close to our apartment, and walked.

My boyfriend was infuriated. I didn't understand why, since he had wasted my entire Saturday. I'd done exactly what he did. We fought like crazy. That switch flipped again, and he began suffocating me with a pillow. I was kicking, and he was using every bit of strength to hold the pillow over my face. I thought he was going to kill me. He was holding me down, choking me, and he was a big, strong guy.

One of our neighbors heard me screaming and called the cops. They arrested us both for domestic violence. The next day, our pictures were plastered all over the television. "Another Police Officer accused of domestic violence!" I was addicted to the dysfunction of this relationship.

*Have you ever been addicted to a dysfunctional relationship? How do you break free of it?*

I didn't know how. The police department's internal affairs office tried to contact me for my side of the story, so they could publicize it on the news. I wouldn't answer the phone. I didn't want my private life out there for everyone to see. My boyfriend had been investigated in the past for previous relationships, so this wasn't his first domestic issue. We had to go to court, and we got everything dismissed.

At that time, a situation with my son's father forced us to move back to North Carolina. My boyfriend wanted to go with me, and I agreed. After the first time he physically abused me, I hadn't set boundaries. That had been a red flag, and I should have ended the relationship then. I was teaching him to treat me badly. In some deranged way, I thought I deserved the abuse. I wasn't secure enough or confident enough to make rational decisions. I didn't know what a healthy relationship looked like. Our reputation was ruined in Savannah, so off we went to another state.

We got a house in the Carolinas and started a new life there. At first, I was the only one working while he tried to find a new career. His police license wouldn't transfer to the Carolinas, and honestly, I don't think he could have been hired after what happened in Georgia. He flopped between jobs. He had dealt with severe depression and had been on medication for more than twenty years.

After the first time he abused me, I insisted he get help for his anger issues. He had been in counseling off and on throughout his life. We even did counseling together. The psychiatrist changed his depression medicine, which I wasn't too happy about. The side effects were bad. So, between the new meds and trying to find a job he liked, it was a challenging time for him.

He was used to having the authority of a police officer. He'd dealt with a lot of drama working in the Carolinas. I agreed to maintain us financially while he figured out what he wanted to do. About a year into our transition, he told me he'd been depressed. "What can I do for you?" I asked. He said, "There's nothing you can do about it, it will subside." I didn't know anything about severe depression, so I figured he'd let me know if he needed me.

Time went on and we had a pretty good life financially and physically, other than his sporadic fits of rage. One Monday morning, I came home from working sixteen hours and as soon as I walked in, he started punching me in the head. I was trying to cover my head, and I was crying, and he just kept punching me. I said, "Why are you doing this to me?"

He stormed out the door and sped off in his car. I was left in turmoil and cried myself to sleep. When he came home later that night, I didn't ask where he'd been. The next day, we didn't talk to each other. On that Wednesday, I told him I wanted out of the relationship. I said, "I'm done! I want out. For five years, I have tolerated abuse from you. Take everything we have. I'll start over!"

"He said, "Just stop!" Later that night, he left a note on the kitchen table. It read "I'm sorry for hitting you. I love you more than anything. I need you, I want you, and I can't live without you. Please don't leave me!"

Thursday came around and we started talking again. We were planning a sixteenth birthday party with the family for my son the following week so I was busy.

Friday, he came home and drank a beer. He was acting super weird, almost like something had taken over his body. He had a calm demeanor. He said, "I'm going to bed early!" I said, "Okay I'm going to my son's ballgame, so I'll be coming to the bedroom to fix up in a few minutes." He got up from the couch quietly and walked slowly to our bedroom. The door shut. A few minutes later, I got up to start getting ready to leave. I went to the bedroom, to find the door locked. I knocked on the door and asked, "Why is this door locked?" No response. I put my ear up to the door and couldn't hear the television. He always left it on when he was in bed. I pushed the door open and found him collapsed behind the door.

My immediate reaction was that he'd had a heart attack. I checked his wrist and no pulse. I grabbed my phone and called 911. The dispatcher asked if I knew CPR. I said, "Yes I do!" He said, "I want you to start CPR on him immediately." I pulled his legs out, and saw a belt wrapped around his neck. I said, "Holy Freak, he hung himself!" At that moment the Emergency Medical Service arrived and immediately began CPR. I was half in shock and half crying hysterically. The EMS workers came to me in the kitchen, and said "You do know we couldn't save him?" I just nodded. I'd watched part of the time they were performing CPR on him, and he was already discolored.

Later, crime scene investigators accessed the situation. My yard was covered with officers. I left with my parents.

The funeral came and went. I spoke with his family quite often following his death and discovered that he'd been diagnosed with Intermittent explosive disorder before I met him. That explained his sporadic fits of rage, why he beat me for no reason.

I cried every day for a year. I wanted to work through my heart ache rather than see a doctor who'd put me on medication. I had so many questions and blamed myself. I wondered if he felt helpless in his diagnosis and wanted to quit hurting me. Maybe suicide was the only way he knew how.

I often wondered if the darkness within me would ever go away. I failed to remember that we can find the light in a dark world. Sometimes our heads are so cluttered, we need to empty them out and start fresh each day. He used to tell me I was an angel sent by God. He loved the way I loved people and wanted to help others. Did he commit suicide because I said I wanted to leave him? My abandonment issues came to haunt me once again. The person I loved so much left me.

That chapter of my life was closed forever, dedicated to the man who felt he was unworthy of living the beautiful life God gave him.

Do you suffer from abandonment issues in your life?
Have you ever been codependent with someone?

# Chapter 5
# THE ABUSE WITHIN

I thought I had escaped the abusers in my life. Had my own body turned on me? I'm waiting at Urgent Care to check on this lump in my breast. The doctor comes in to tell me that she thinks it's my breast implants, and it's nothing to worry about. I sigh in relief.

Time goes on, and the lump gets considerably bigger. I see the doctor several more times, only to hear the same thing, "It's your implants, you should really see a plastic surgeon." I call a plastic surgeon. He wants my surgery records, but it's almost impossible to get them.

One spring morning, my breast is so hard and discolored, I take myself to the emergency room. They perform an ultrasound and set me up to see a breast cancer surgeon. I ask the nurse advocate, "Do I have cancer?" She says, "Oh Honey, this doctor deals with other things besides cancer." I feel she's hiding something.

As soon as the oncologist sees my breast, she says," I'm a straight shooter. I tell it like it is."

I say, "Just tell me, I've been in healthcare for more than fifteen years. I can handle it."

"You have cancer. We're going to do some biopsies to identify what kind it is."

Tears stream down my face. She performs the biopsies, and I'm in excruciating pain, but they give me meds to help with that.

About a week later, the doctor calls me with the results. "You have Stage 3b inflammatory breast cancer. We need to act fast. This is the most aggressive type."

I'm lost for words, and horrified. I did everything right—doctors' appointments, oncology visits. I didn't know what to expect. I was always one to research everything, but when I researched my cancer, I was even more frightened. The typical life span of someone with Stage 3b is less than five years. Within a couple of years, it usually metastasizes to the bones and organs.

The week before I began chemotherapy, we traveled the Northeast. I knew I wouldn't be able to do much after I started treatment, and I wanted to make some memories with my sons. We went to Portland and Old Orchard Beach, Maine; Boston, Massachusetts; Newport and Providence Rhode Island. We had a great time exploring and stayed at some nice places. In Maine, we went to Acadia National Park, where we made a campfire and cooked hotdogs and s'mores, and one night, we went out for lobster. It was my younger son's first time on an airplane, and I was excited about that.

The doctors tell me I have a 20% chance of living five years. My boys are with me at my first chemotherapy appointment. The nurse gowns up, puts a face shield on, and fills three 20cc syringes with a red liquid. She says they called it "The Red Devil." She slowly injects each syringe into my port.

My oldest son sits with me for hours while I get the infusion. I can feel the chemotherapy traveling through my body, eating out my insides. It's unlike anything I've ever felt. I figure, if this is going to kill my cancer, I'd better go through with it.

I'm okay for a couple of days, then I get weaker and weaker, until I can't get out of bed. If I try to eat or drink, I regurgitate. My son tries everything to help, but I can barely move. I cry and tell him how proud of him I am. It's a defining moment for me, because he says, "Mom why do all your friends say you're so strong? It's because you are, and you're stubborn. I get my stubbornness from you. You can do it, Mom!" It's the motivational speech I need.

My son had been in Germany during his spring break, and he was going back to study there in the fall. I was so proud of him, twenty years old and trying to take care of me. My younger son was the little tough guy. He said, "Mom is a bad ass. She'll get through it!"

The next day, I force myself out of bed. I barely make it down the stairs and start eating applesauce. It tastes so good. I was starving. My son asks if I'm feeling better." I say, "Yeah, I got this!"

After that, I was always down the third day after chemotherapy. The doctors gave me a patch to wear after chemo to keep my white blood cell count from bottoming out, and it helped a lot. Chemo was the worst thing I ever encountered. There were moments when I fell to my knees and cried out, "Please God, just take me!" And every time, I heard a voice telling me to get up. People are watching you. You're going to be okay.

I don't understand why life dealt me this hand, but Christ was leading me to my revelation. Many times, I was so weak, I had to crawl to the bathroom. The neuropathy in my feet caused problems with walking, and sometimes I had to use a cane.

I forced myself to exercise even if it was only talking a walk somewhere. For some reason, I craved ice cream. One day, when I went out for some, I forgot my headwrap. Everyone stared at my bald head and allowed me to cut in front of them in line. I just smiled and ordered my ice cream, but inside, it really bothered me.

Why were these people judging me by my outward appearance? Then a moment of clarity came to me: For thirty-eight years of my life, I'd judged people. This required self-evaluation.

Do you judge people?
Do you feel unworthy of living the wholesome life God
intended for you?
Why do we judge people when we are as imperfect
as anyone else?

After four months of chemotherapy, my tumor only shrank from fifteen to fourteen centimeters. All that misery hadn't even helped. The doctors decided that an operation was next on the list. I took a week off to spend time with my family before surgery. I had a great time going to an NFL game with one son and international soccer game with the other, and I had a lot of family dinners.

I'd undergo surgery in another state. My family wasn't keen on that, but I was doing it alone. A friend took me to the hospital that morning. In the operating room, I'm hooked up to IV's and the nurse says she's giving me a little something to relax. That's the last thing I remember.

While performing a mastectomy with a tram flap reconstruction, the doctor accidentally punctured my lungs causing a pneumothorax and pulmonary embolism. Was God giving me what I'd begged him for? Was I dying? I was drifting away. My soul was leaving my body. I felt it.

Four days later, I felt a force push me back into the world and I woke up. What happened to me while I was in a coma? I felt I had been given an assignment. Was this God? Was this my revelation? When I woke up, I couldn't move my arms. I was paralyzed. I asked the nurse to text my sons, to tell them that I was okay, and that I loved them.

I was in tremendous pain. I was connected to tons of intravenous lines. I know I was getting morphine, a blood transfusion, and anticoagulants, but I had no idea what else they were giving me. I hit that morphine button every chance I could. The nurses had to feed me and do everything for me. I was too weak to do anything for myself.

During the day, doctors came in and out of my room. One day a cardiologist came to tell me he was putting me on heart medications, and I said I wouldn't do it. My heart rate was constant at about 150 bpm, but I didn't have a heart condition. My problem was caused by the doctor who punctured my lung. I told her that while I was on oxygen, gasping for every breath. I could barely talk but I knew what they were doing to me. I had been an avid runner for about twenty years. I knew my heart was in excellent condition.

I'd had an echocardiogram showing that my heart was at eighty percent both before and after the chemo, which was unheard of. I had always been a healthy person. My family gave me grief about taking so many supplements, and I'd jokingly retort, "I'll probably be the first to expire since I take all this." I tried to find humor even in the worst situations.

I got into a yelling match with the cardiologist, and he left the room. When a nurse came in, I told her to write "No heart meds" on my chart. Who were they trying to fool? Hopefully, not me. I wouldn't accept their nonsense, keeping me medicated until my body wore out. I was going to fight with every ounce of my being. I had to remember I had a family outside that hospital who needed me as much as I needed them.

For five and a half weeks, I went through the same monotonous routine. The doctors came in every morning to check on me. They listened to my lungs, checked my oxygen levels, my drainage tubes and so forth. I swear it seemed like at least ten doctors came in my room every morning. The pulmonary doctor, the cardiologist, plastic surgeon, breast surgeon... the list goes on. Physical therapy was scheduled daily. If they didn't show up, I complained. I wanted to get better. I wanted to go home. I remained positive even though I suspected that the doctors didn't expect me to leave that hospital alive.

A friend from another state flew in to see me, bringing me pajamas. The next day, she left abruptly with an excuse she later admitted was a lie. She said, "I couldn't stand seeing you like that, girl. I thought you were going to die." I told her I understood. I'd heard that several times from former coworkers who visited me. I must have looked bad.

One day a volunteer came to my room and asked, "Honey, what kinds of things do you like to do?" Instantly I replied, "I love to color!" Later that evening, she came back with coloring books and a huge pack of colored pencils. I will be forever grateful to that woman. I never got her name, and I don't think she knows how much that meant to me.

People who come into our lives, even for a moment, can change the way we view the world.

*Have you ever had an encounter with someone who changed you? Do you ever feel empathetic toward someone going through a difficult time, whether it's an ailment or life circumstance?*

I had been hired at a prestigious medical hospital known for treating cancer in another state. I had to get out of the hospital in order to take the job.

After about four and half weeks, the hospital tried to discharge me. My insurance had lapsed, and my medical bills were accumulating. If the hospital wasn't getting paid, they wanted me out. My chest was still split wide open, and the wound was necrotic, so I was hooked up to a vac.

The financial advisor came to tell me I was being discharged. I said, "I'm septic. I'll die if I go home. I need medication and care."

She said, "I'm sorry but you don't have insurance. We can try to set you up with assistance outside the hospital."

"Ma'am, if you discharge me, and something happens to me, this hospital will be liable"

I was so upset, my heart rate went up. She stormed out of the room, and my nurse came in.

"Girl, what happened in here? Your doctor and the financial director are arguing in the hallway."

I was still on about forty percent oxygen and gasping for every breath. I said, "That lady is trying to discharge me. In the condition I'm in, I'll freaking die! I can't go home like this."

A few minutes later, my doctor came and said, "Don't worry about anything. We're going to get you better!" At least I felt like my surgeons were on my side now, although they almost killed me during the surgery.

The hospital moved me to a nursing home. I agreed to that. I was getting better but the wound vac was still in my chest. I would have a little more access to things and the transport service would take me to my appointments to see the doctors. I met a wonderful lady there who was in her seventies. We talked every day and had coffee together. I think she told me more about her personal life than her own family knew. I got her number and we tried to stay in touch.

As we go through life, it's hard to stay in touch with everyone we meet. Some people are meant to stay in our lives for a season, perhaps they are there when we need help. I needed that lady, although she didn't know it. I'll bet she needed me, too.

Have you ever met someone for a moment, and later realized that you got something out of it?
Perhaps, you learned a valuable lesson, or it was a defining moment that changed the way you thought about something.

In the nursing home, I was allowed to have visitors. Friends who had my car parked it in the lot so I could leave when they discharged me. December came. The temperatures were dropping, and it was snowing. I was anxious to know when I'd get out of there.

39

They sewed my chest up and discharged me. I told them that as soon as I got to the next state, I'd see a doctor there. A friend packed my car for me. She bought vacuum bags and sealed up all my clothes. Every day after I was discharged, she came to my house to help me. She was my rock! I hope she is reading this story so I can express my gratitude to her and to all the girls I worked with who came to see me and brought me things. I was so paralyzed and felt so helpless and these young ladies improved my life in so many ways.

My chest began to bleed profusely, and the doctor told me to come to his office before I left the state. He cut a few stitches in my chest and packed the incision with gauze. He told me to clean and pack it until I got to the next doctor.

I drove fifteen hours, stopping every hour to jog in place so I wouldn't get another blood clot. Several times, I had to pull over at rest areas, inject myself with the anticoagulant Lovenox and pack and clean my chest wound.

When I finally reached my destination, I went to the home of a friend who also worked in the medical field. When I showed her my chest wound, she said, "It smells like you have a staph infection brewing in there." I couldn't have agreed with her more. The stench was horrendous, and the drainage was almost intolerable.

She took me to the hospital emergency department. When they heard my story, they were so amazed that I was alive to talk about it, they presented my case all over the city and every specialist got involved. They cut more stitches in my chest and drained it. I had a staph infection, an anaerobic infection, and I was septic.

I called my older son. "Mom, just come home!" He must have thought I was going to die, and wanted to be with me, but I wasn't giving up. I said, "I promise you. I'm going to be okay. Please trust me and let me do what I have to do now." He was trying so hard to be supportive. I'd been hospitalized for six weeks and I was far from my family, but I knew if I didn't keep pushing forward I'd lose the war with cancer.

40

Cancer Is the leading cause of death worldwide. Every year, more than 1.6 million people are diagnosed with cancer and over 600,000 die. I was determined to win this fight. So many people were following my story on social media. I had received cards, letters, and messages supporting me in this fight.

Another thing that kept me going was my belief that while I was in a coma, I had been given a test. I wasn't sure what it meant, but I knew it meant something. There was something bigger in this world for me. I knew I wasn't going to die. I knew this would end and a beautiful chapter of my life would begin. My faith in a higher power would get me through this.

*Have you ever thought you were destined to become something, but the world was against you?*
*Write down a moment or a time when your family or someone you loved was against you.*
*How did that make you feel?*
*Were you able to overcome it or did you just forget about yourself?*

During this time, I had an argument with a friend. She said, "Go home and be with your family. You're dying!"

I said, "No, I'm not. I know you don't believe in God, but I do, and I promise you, He's not done with me yet!"

We were both crying and yelling at each other in the hospital. She told the doctor that if they discharged me, I'd to go to work. The doctor looked at me in astonishment not knowing what to say. They kept me for a couple days, and yes, I started a new job that required travel.

My friend said, "How are you going to work with your chest half open, giving yourself injections in the stomach every day?"

My response: "Life is always going to throw curve balls, but you have to adjust to your circumstances and keep fighting!" I needed a job and medical insurance. My mother taught me never to give up on anything. She was tough. She taught us to keep pushing forward. I went to work and continued my life.

I tried to make an appointment with the oncologist where I worked, but my request was denied because I hadn't received my insurance card yet. I broke down crying. "I'm dying," I said, "I need to see a doctor!" All they cared about was making sure they got paid. I'd worked in healthcare my entire life. Now that I was a patient, I didn't think I should be treated so badly. What a disgrace!

One of the doctors helped me find a nurse advocate who began setting me up with the care I needed. I fought a lot. I was a force to be reckoned with. The doctor I saw wanted to operate again to remove the remaining cancer cells, but I was still healing from the surgery I'd had two months before. I refused and held my ground.

Once again, I was in a yelling match with a surgeon. Finally, I agreed to a biopsy. If it came back positive, I would rethink my decision. When the results came back, no cancer was found. The doctors said that was impossible. I'd been diagnosed with Stage 3b and after surgery, I'd went to Stage 4. They'd told me that the cancer was all in my lymph nodes and that although they'd removed sixteen, they hadn't gotten it all. They gave me six months to live.

Now the surgeon said, "It's impossible. You still have cancer. You can't have stage four cancer and then no cancer anywhere!"

I said, "Do you believe in God?"

He looked at me like I was an idiot. I walked out of that office and went to another doctor. He said," How do you feel about going back for more surgery?"

I said, "Sir I don't agree with it. They did a biopsy, and it came back negative. I haven't even healed from the surgery I underwent two months ago. I'm still immunocompromised. My body can't handle it."

He said, "I couldn't agree with you more.

I was so relieved. One person was on my side.

He said, "That's why we have a team of doctors here. We can confer on the best mode of treatment for you going forward."

A couple of days later, they decide to start radiation. I underwent forty-eight treatments. Every morning, I reported for radiation, then off to work I went. Radiation wasn't that bad. The technicians were nice, and at my last treatment, they played the song, "Hit the Road Jack."

Yes, I wanted to hit the road and never come back again. I was a little tired, but I felt that my body was getting healthier. That year I underwent two more surgeries, and by the end of 2019, I was feeling good. In 2020, I was in complete remission, and it felt great.

Sometimes when I woke up, my body just hurt. Occasionally, I'd see my scarred body in the mirror and tears streamed down my face. I wondered if anyone would want me like this. I was on the road to self-discovery. How could I get past what I saw in the mirror? I was broken inside, and now I looked broken outside, as well.

Have you ever looked in the mirror and seen only your flaws?
Do you ever wonder who could love you with all your imperfections?
Why do we have such a negative perception of ourselves?
Do you lack self-awareness?
Can you turn a tragedy into a victory?

In 2021, I wasn't feeling well, and I took myself to the doctor. My yearly mammogram came back negative for cancer, but I didn't believe it, so I got a second opinion in another state. An MRI came back with abnormal lymph nodes and cancer in my chest cavity. The doctors wanted to operate to remove the cancer. It would be surgery number eight in four years.

The operation was unsuccessful. The doctor told me, " Heather, I hate saying what I am about to say, but during surgery we were unable to remove all the cancer cells. Cancer is eating you up, and all we can offer you is additional chemotherapy in the hope that you'll live a little longer."

My response disturbed him. I said, "Okay, no problem. "

He looked at me puzzled and said, "I just told you there's nothing more we can do for you. Why are you so calm about it? Either you have a really good poker face or you're dying inside."

Two nurse advocates were in the room. I looked at the doctor and said, "Sir, I have a strong faith in God, and I know He has me either way. I'm going to be okay."

He said, "Fair enough," and left the office. He seemed more disheartened than I did. I'd already known the results of the surgery. I'd been praying for God's guidance.

My cousin told me of an experimental treatment protocol, and I reached out to a doctor who used it. He reviewed all my medical records and said he thought he could help me, but that there were no guarantees. I made arrangements to fly down to see him. In September of 2021, I began the new treatment regimen, and so far, I'm doing well.

We are always capable of more than we think we are, and our minds are our greatest healing tool.

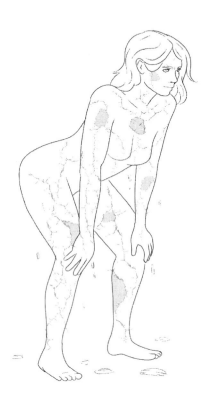

# Chapter 6
# OUT OF THE TOMB

How do we know that a higher power exists?
Who is God? Is God an omnipresent, supernatural being?
Why do people talk about this book called the Bible?
God has been talked about for more than three thousand years
and we still talk about God today.
What is the purpose of life?
Can a higher power disclose the truth?

When I was in a coma, I saw my spirit leave my body, and I heard God speaking to me. When I regained consciousness, I felt I had been given an assignment. I didn't mention it to anyone at the time, because I didn't know what it meant, but believing in a higher power meant surrendering myself to faith. How do you get to a point when you can surrender your will and your thoughts, ideas and deeds to a higher power?

The religious cult I grew up in gave me a distorted perception of who God was. I couldn't understand how my father, a pedophile, could be saved by God. The Bible tells us Jesus was crucified on the cross for our sins. The cross signifies the redeeming nature of his passion and that he experienced human pain for us. God the Father sent his son Jesus to atone for us.

I was on a mission to read the Bible and develop my own understanding of who God was. I was often asked, "Why does God allow horrible things to happen if he is loving?"

The twenty-four books of the Old Testament are divided into Law, History, Poetry, and Prophets. The books concerning Law were written by Moses whom God called to be his prophet and to lead the Israelites out of Egypt. He describes the creation and the Jews wandering in the wilderness. The books concerning History record the events of the nation of Israel.

The books of Poetry include the story of Job who lost everything he had. God told him to trust Him and have faith, but Satan told Job to turn his back on God. When he refused, God blessed him with more than he could have imagined.

The prophetic books of the Old Testament bring a message of hope and future blessings if we walk the path of obedience. As I read the Old Testament, I wondered, "How does this relate to my life now?"

The New Testament describes the covenant between man and God through Christ. We are told it was written by a number of people many years after the death of Jesus, so how do we know there is truth in it? In the New Testament, some of Jesus's twelve disciples write their versions of the Gospel, describing how He showed them what was in store for them. Judas, one of the disciples, turned his back on Jesus. In John 13:21, Jesus says, "Truly, truly I say unto you that one of you will betray me." The disciples looked at each other. "In John 13:26 Jesus says, "It is the one to whom I will give this piece of bread when I have dipped it in the dish.' Then, dipping the piece of bread, he gave it to Judas, the son of Simon Iscariot."

God has taken me through many trials and tribulations. These shaped my interpretation of Him and brought me to my ultimate revelation. God tells us that when we live for the world, we fail to live for Him. When I was in a coma, I decided to surrender to His spirit and have faith that a higher power existed, to allow Him to direct my life. I had to shift my focus and change my perspective, to accept that I could be something more after this life.

In Romans 15:4, Jesus says, "Whatever was written in earlier times was written for our instruction, so that through perseverance and the encouragement of the Scriptures we might have hope." In the New Testament the disciples show us the works of Jesus with those who had faith in him. If there really is a God, then he will give me direction in all aspects of my life so long as I have faith in him.

Most Christians think about Jesus dying on the cross for our sins, but more importantly, the Bible tells us that he arose from the grave three days later. and that is what gave us grace. Mark 16:6 reads, "And he said to them, 'Do not be amazed, you are looking for Jesus the Nazarene who has been crucified. He is risen. He is not here; behold, here is the place where they laid him.'"

Grace is the free and unmerited favor given to us by God. We are all sinners in this imperfect world, but through grace and faith we admit that we need a savior. I think we are each led to our own revelation.

I began to allow my faith in Jesus to direct my life. I felt the spirit leading me to where I needed to go. I surrendered and began to believe that Jesus did exist and that He would guide me.

It was such an amazing feeling. I knew without a doubt that I would survive cancer. Doctors and friends told me I was going to die, and I told them that God wasn't done with me yet. I can't explain the feeling or how I knew, but when you have your revelation in life and really surrender yourself to the spirit of Jesus, it's unlike anything you've ever felt.

Matthew 21:22 reads, "Whatever you ask in prayer, you will receive." It doesn't mean If you ask for a new car, you'll get it. It simply means that when you ask for guidance and direction in your life, God will give it to you. It didn't mean that my life would be perfect. I was going through a very challenging time, but I knew if I had faith in God, no matter what obstacles I came across, He would get me through it.

Hebrews 11:1 reads, "And without faith it is impossible to please Him, for whoever would draw near to God must believe He exists, and that He rewards those who seek him." Growing up in a dysfunctional family, I had so many questions about God. As a child, my perception of God was defined by the religious cult I lived in. I couldn't grasp what I read in the Bible. My father recited Bible verses that justified his sinful ways. I thought in order to be a Christian, I had to vow never to curse, or drink, or have sex outside marriage, and so on.

The Bible never tells us not to drink alcohol. Galatians 5:19-21 reads: "The acts of the sinful nature are obvious... drunkenness, orgies, and the like. I warn you, as I did before, that those who live like this will not inherit the kingdom of God." The Bible never says not to drink because it's tainted by sin. It just says that getting drunk is not living for Christ.

I realized that we are all sinners. Romans 12:2 reads "And do not be conformed to this world, but be transformed by the renewing of your mind, so that you may prove what the will of God is, that which is good and acceptable and perfect." As I continued to read the Bible, it answered so many of my questions about God. I know that these words were written centuries ago, but if they were true then, isn't God the same as he has always been?

I know that faith and religion are subjective, but as I continued to read the Bible, the statement became clear. I prayed and sought God to help me gain knowledge, and Christ's prophetic words made sense to me.

As I continue to get closer to God, He gives me a glimpse of things to come, just as He did for the twelve apostles. I can't imagine my life today without my savior. I will continue to live every day for God and I thank him every day for allowing me to receive my revelation. God transformed the tragedy of cancer into my greatest testimony.

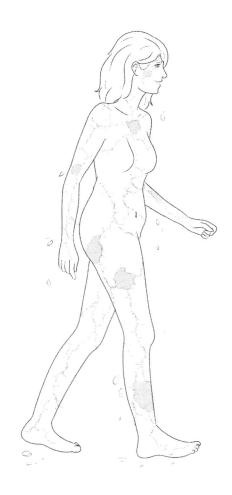

# Chapter 7
# NO REGRETS

Our confidence in ourselves gives us value. Growing up in an abusive home, I developed toxic qualities. As a child, I saw my parents in an abusive marriage and learned that behavior. We are programmed to see our parents as our protectors and nurturers. When we experience abuse, it distorts our perception of what love is and how it is shown to us. When I saw my father abuse my mother, knowing they were supposed to love each other, I thought that abuse was an expression of love.

In therapy, I learned that my father's toxic behavior had been wired into my brain, and that I was programmed to unconsciously look for similar qualities in the men I dated. My parents set me up for failure without realizing it. As we go through life, we must decide whether our misfortunes will define or inspire us.

Accepting the pain I experienced and forgiving those who hurt me are the greatest gifts I have given myself. My therapist taught me that I had to reprogram my mind to think differently. She explained that I needed to put myself in situations that might be uncomfortable in order to train myself to see things differently.

Nearly one in seven girls is abused before her eighteenth birthday. When my biological father passed away, my son asked me how I felt about it. I didn't feel anything. He caused my family so much turmoil it felt surreal. The darkness he left behind will forever live within us all. The trauma my brothers lived with is indescribable.

I had to go through challenging times in order to see that my purpose is to help young women learn to love themselves, even through the hard times. Loving yourself is looking in the mirror every day and knowing that you deserve to be loved. It is knowing that you deserve to be treated with dignity and respected. Self-love is taking care of your own needs, rather than sacrificing your wellbeing to appease others. It is appreciating yourself and placing importance on your own happiness.

My research showed that domestic abuse happens to "an average of twenty people per minute in the United States." That equates to ten million people who are abused in one year. Why do we stay with someone who abuses us?

I stayed because I grew up thinking that abuse meant he loved me. I thought I could change him. I wanted to be loved just like anyone else. I was afraid to be alone. My abusers made me feel that I needed them.

As a single parent, I thought I couldn't survive by myself, so I stayed for financial reasons. How could I break away from the mentality I grew up with, believing those toxic behaviors were acceptable? I had to change the way I thought. I deserved better. I had to learn to love myself first, even though it felt uncomfortable. I had to change my entire mindset. I could choose to change through pain and suffering and learn in joy and inspiration. or I could keep repeating this toxic cycle. Once I began practicing mindfulness, changing my mindset got easier.

When you wake up every day, you can decide to allow yourself to be treated like the queen you are. You're worth it! I've realized that we all want some of the same things. We all want to be loved, feel wanted, be successful, and enjoy life.

I began to ponder the meaning of success. Each of us measures success differently. Is success being able to work through every challenge you come across? Is success being financially stable? For me, success is a progressive understanding of a worthy goal. Science says that 95% of people are unsuccessful because they get up and go to work every day without having a goal in mind. They repeat a monotonous routine day after day, year after year.

Napoleon Hill said, "Successful people make decisions promptly and change these decisions slowly if they are changed at all. Unsuccessful people make decisions very slowly and change them quickly and often."

One day my mother asked me," When are you going to be content with life?" My response was, "When I complete this task. Then I want to do this and that." For a few years, I thought about that question often. She was right in a sense. She said, "You're never going to be content in life if you keep making goals for yourself and achieving them is the only thing that will make you happy."

I realized that I had a vision of what I wanted to happen in my future. I could either create that vision or keep living in my past. After you experience trauma, you anticipate worst case scenarios in anything you do, and that conditions your body to fear. You become addicted to the rush of emotions you unconsciously created. I decided I could either live as a victim or become the producer of my world and live in reality. If we get stuck thinking of the past, we get caught in a whirlwind of emotions. So how do we get past that?

For me, the key was meditation. Every day, I practiced meditation for about ten minutes, disconnecting from my environment. Eventually, the past became no more than a memory, and I was able to live in the moment. Meditation brings buried traumatic memories to your conscious mind. When I became aware of them, I could begin to deal with them, and to heal.

When I found an outlet for my traumatic memories and built-up emotions, I was able to recreate my life. Once I started healing and living in the moment, my anxiety ceased. I was able to stay more focused on the task at hand. Everything In my life seemed clearer. I wasn't fixated on past hurt, but looked back on my past relationships and saw clearly how broken I'd been.

I always found broken people like me. I felt a connection and I could feel their pain. When I started to heal, I began to see beyond outward appearances and sensed the hurt in others.

I always wondered why God allowed bad things to happen to good people. But I realized that however horrible my cancer was, it taught me valuable lessons. Cancer taught me strength. The old saying "You don't know how strong you are until being strong is your only option" was so true for me. Cancer taught me that God is miraculous and that my faith in Him has kept me alive.

People around me didn't believe in God, but I kept telling them, "God isn't done with me yet." They laughed and ridiculed me, but here I am today, sharing my testimony with the world. Cancer taught me that the things we stress about every day are trivial.

When you're facing death and the neuropathy in your feet and legs is so bad you have to crawl to the bathroom, getting stressed because someone at work spoke badly of you seems ridiculous.

We are in control of our own destinies. Every day we can choose to become the person we strive to be, the person God is preparing us to become. The degree to which we prosper corresponds with the degree of truth we are willing to accept about ourselves.

In 2018 when I was diagnosed with cancer, my roommate at the time gave me a session with a master of Reiki, a Japanese method of healing. I had no idea what it was, but she told me to be open minded. I've always been fascinated with learning new things, especially any type of natural healing. The Reiki master talked with me for almost an hour. She asked about some of the things that were bothering me and the pain and hurt from my past. Then she asked me to stretch out on her table while she described the seven chakras and told me that when they are blocked, they cause problems.

This verbiage was foreign to me. She talked about parts of the body, and redirecting my energy. Tears streamed down my face and my stomach felt as though aliens were coming out of it. It was the weirdest experience I ever had.

After the session was over, she asked," Have you ever thought of someone when suddenly, they call you?" I said, "Yes." She said that is because you were transferring energy to the other person. I got into my car and was thinking of calling my son when my phone rang. I told him all about it.

I felt better, but I wasn't sure why, so I began to research Reiki healing. I found that it's a natural healing process and spiritual practice dating back 2500 years, which was rediscovered in Japan in the 1920s. I started getting my chakras balanced periodically and practicing Reiki, as well.

I had been in and out of therapy since I got married at the age of twenty, but when I had sessions with my husband, the therapist irritated me. I was so broken and in denial. In therapy, I was told that because I was the youngest, the things I witnessed as a child affected me more than my older siblings. I thought that was nonsense but later learned that the abuse had affected me more than I'd imagined, that it had distorted my perception of "normal" behavior. I had no way of knowing what love was or how to be loved, or that no one ever has the right to hurt you or control you in any way.

During therapy, I discovered I wasn't at fault for anything that happened to me as a child. I was innocent, vulnerable, helpless and only wanted to be a little girl. I'd packed all those emotions deep inside. Then, with every abusive relationship, I packed away more hurt, until I hit bottom and couldn't do it anymore.

One day I realized I was spinning out of control. I had to open myself up to heal. I had to be transparent and realize my scars don't define who I am. I had to move beyond the pain and hurt to be able to help others who were going through the same thing. There's truth in the saying, "Life is understood backward and lived forward." I was trying to understand why I had gone through so many trials and tribulations, why I was denied the peace of knowing that God was bringing me to my ultimate revelation.

Forgiveness isn't about the people who hurt us. We forgive others so that we can heal. I went through a process of releasing the psychological and emotional damage I'd been carrying around for years. I finally came to a point when I could no longer escape the past. The past has already occurred, and I can't predict the future. I'm living in the present.

It is so easy to get caught up in thinking you need a backup plan for everything. I put all my trust in God, knowing that He is guiding my life. It's great to be responsible, but I had to realize that life happens daily. When I understood that I couldn't prevent things that were beyond my control, life seemed easier.

I decided to stay away from people who were toxic for me, bad for my mental health. Sometimes that meant my own family. I had to heal first. I had to put myself before anyone else. I'd always tried hard to please my family. I never spoke up or told anyone how I felt, and that left me heartbroken. I was carrying around everyone else's problems, trying to fix everyone around me, when I needed to fix myself. I'd done that for so long, it was hard to put myself first.

I'm not exactly where I want to be at this point in my life, but I've never been happier. I'm so confident about where I am in life, so secure with myself. I know that what I've been through is just part of my story.

*How do you handle stress?*
*Do you prepare for things that never happen?*

When a frightening thought crossed my mind, I'd dissect it. For example, If I was worried that my cancer was metastasizing, I'd ask myself, "Why am I worried about that?" My answer was that I wasn't ready to die yet. So then I asked myself, "Why does that mean, 'I'm dying?' What if I *was* dying, what would I do?" The answer I came up with was that if my cancer had spread and the doctors told me I was dying, as they did in 2018, I wouldn't go home and twiddle my thumbs waiting to die. Absolutely not.

We cause every bit of stress in our lives. Statistics have shown that 85% of the things we worry about never happen. Live your life being present in the moment. Confidence is instilled in us at a young age, but it can become distorted. First, we must become aware of insecurities, and then we need to want to lose them.

We can choose to be inspired or defined by anything that happens to us. I couldn't change being abused as a child, but I could change the way I dealt with it. I couldn't change having cancer, but I could change my attitude toward it. I could change feeling insecure as a result of my childhood trauma. I could change that learned behavior of thinking all people are psychopaths like my father. I could change my job, my wealth, my knowledge, my surroundings, but I had to want to put in the effort to do those things.

So many people just accept the cards they're dealt and allow that to define who they are in this world. You have to create your world and your environment. I've survived one hundred percent of what life has thrown at me. Cancer is just part of my story. Everything I've endured in life has resulted in the current version of me.

I went through really low times, and that made me resilient.

I lost everything and that made me appreciative.

God gave me strength even when I didn't think I had any. I was fearful of the future until I realized it was up to me to get what I wanted.

Don't be afraid to accept rejection, because that makes us stronger.
Don't be afraid to lose someone, because you could lose
yourself in the process.
If someone doesn't put you first in their life, don't magnify
your place in it.
Your life is about outgrowing yourself.
Don't compare your life with anyone else's.

Make your future better than your past.
Giving yourself more may seem selfish, but if you don't, you'll have
nothing to give anyone else.
Have a healthy respect for yourself and shift your focus to the
things you want in life, instead of the things you don't want.

Psychologists suggest that 80% of families are dysfunctional. I was amazed to see such a high percentage. It's sad to know that there are so many others like myself.

Make room for your desires.
Focus on your dreams and visions.
Opportunities are endless if you search for them.
Attend to things that make you joyous whatever they may be. Listen
to music that makes you happy.

According to a school of psychology in Australia, recent studies have demonstrated increased activity in brain regions associated with emotion and reward when listening to pleasurable music. Numerous neuroscientists measured brain waves showing that people can heal themselves with their mindsets alone, whether it's the placebo affect or sound therapy. I've always found that listening to worship music or happy songs brings me a sense of peace.

Learn to be alone and love yourself in the process.
Find hobbies you enjoy and never look to others for happiness.

When I was younger, one of my biggest mistakes was thinking that other people brought me happiness or completed me. I was so broken, I didn't love myself at all. In my search for a life partner, I took the toxicity of my childhood into every relationship. And I didn't give myself time to heal between relationships.

# Chapter 8
# LIVE OR RISK IT ALL

Time is a limited currency.
What does time mean to you?
How do you value time?
How does God want you to spend your time here on earth?

As my stepfather got older, he'd occasionally mention that he'd always wanted to go to Alaska, but that flying and changing planes would be too hard for him. Several times, I told him that I would pay for us all to go. We'd put him in a wheelchair and get first class service, but he thought he was too old and fragile. I had a job that allowed me to travel anywhere. I decided to work in Alaska so he could see it through pictures.

My mom always joked that I should quit traveling and live my life through pictures on the internet. I didn't like my job in Alaska and left after a couple of months, but I was able to show my stepfather how beautiful it was.

I was up for a new work assignment, and I talked to him about a few of my options. He wanted me to go to Wyoming. He'd enjoyed watching the old Western movies with Clint Eastwood, so I wasn't surprised that Wyoming was on his bucket list. While I was in Wyoming, he passed away. I was glad that I'd been able to fulfil some of his wishes.

Sadly, most people fear the unknown. When I was younger, I thought time was about checking off my bucket list, but as I got older and went through cancer, I had a spiritual awakening and realized that every day I woke up was a blessing. I began to value time. Time management is the capital we invest in ourselves. If we invest in relationships, money, homes, cars, and other things, how does that help us prosper?. When we die, we can't take any of the physical things with us. But we leave behind the memories we make with the people we love.

It's about making an impact on the lives of others, whether they're strangers or family. I've realized that everyone is fighting a battle I know nothing about. We're all battling every day. The more I travel and the more people I meet, the more I realize how many people are broken. I get to hear their stories, learn how their lives have been impacted and the challenges they've faced. I feel their sadness and emptiness, and I want to help.

What do you value in life?
Every day when we wake up, we have a limited amount of time, and we choose how to fill it.

When I was younger and a single parent, I thought it was important that my son had all the things he wanted. I made sure he was always involved in sports. One day when he was older, he said, "Mom I didn't care about all that stuff you bought me or the sports I played, I just wanted quality time with you." I was pleasantly surprised, but I had done the whole parenthood thing wrong. I thought making sure my son had everything he wanted was part of being a parent. I thought that having him involved in every sport possible was giving him opportunities I never had, because my parents were busy working to support me. I realized that staying home on a Friday night to play Monopoly was more important to him than going out to a fancy restaurant.

Why did I have this perception that spending money showed my kids I loved them? Maybe because before she remarried my step-father, my mom was gone all the time working three jobs trying to support me and my sister, so she bought us things to compensate. Did she feel guilty for not being around, or was that how she expressed her love? Either way, I learned that behavior.

As I became an adult and began working on myself in therapy, I realized I couldn't continue to torture myself for not knowing how to be a parent. All I could do was go with the knowledge I had and do the best I knew how at that moment in my life. I don't think I'm the only parent who felt that way. Talking with other women, I've learned that we have a lot of obligations. We're expected to care for the kids, work, cook dinner, clean the house and many other things, so we often neglect ourselves.

The biggest mistake we make in life is thinking we have more time. Everyday over one hundred and fifty thousand people die around the world, and I'd bet that the majority of them didn't see it coming. At an early age, I experienced the death of loved ones, including my brother who was murdered when he was only twen-ty-four. When you're young, you never expect things like that to happen. Later, you realize that death is inevitable.

After a friend passed away, Albert Einstein said, "Time is an illusion." What did he mean by that? For a busy individual, an hour might seem like ten minutes, but to an idle person, ten hours might seem like days. Time is free. You can't own it, but once it's lost, you can never get it back.

Sometimes we don't get second chances to say "I'm sorry" or "I love you." The way you manage your time is up to you, but you can't keep it and it will run out. It will eventually end for us all.

Remember that both good times and bad are temporary. When life is good, enjoy it to the fullest. Live in the moment.

One of the things that keeps people from living in the moment is social media. I love photographing every moment, but that keeps me from being present. Over three billion people in the world are on social media. My stepfather hated social media and cell phones. He used to comment that we needed to leave all electronic devices outside before entering his house. Social media is great for keeping in touch with long distance family and networking for jobs. A lot of women get affirmation by posting beautiful pictures. It's great to feel good about yourself and receive compliments. But social media is no way to gain confidence or find affirmation. Social media should be used to impact people rather than impress them. Studies show that people average more than thirteen hundred hours a year on social media. They average six hundred hours a year watching Netflix. I'm not saying that relaxing in front of the TV is bad, but what if you spent all those hours accomplishing something you wanted? We spend most of our time doing absolutely nothing.

I chose to use my time wisely. After I surrendered myself to God, I realized that it's okay to go out and be bold and enjoy the things you want. I wanted to be a speaker for God. I wanted to show people what Christ had done in my life. I believe if we go through life without purpose, we miss the point of living. I decided to exchange some of my gratification for the security of Christ.

### WHAT DO YOU THINK YOUR PURPOSE IS IN LIFE?
Can you live life to the fullest with purpose?

When I came close to death, I began to understand what time meant to me. I saw it slowly passing by, day after day, year after year. I have chosen to live my life to the fullest for God. I value every minute of every day I'm alive. I make sure to enjoy the things in this world and to keep Christ in my life every day.

I wake up and realize my heart is still beating. I've gotten through some of my darkest days, but I'm still breathing. It's not a mistake that I'm still alive and you are, too. We have an unmerited amount of favor and grace with God. Sometimes a delay in something could mean God's protection. I love the quote, "Don't live the same year seventy-five times and call it a life." We get so scared to venture away from the monotonous routine we've been taught and discover what the world is really like. When you discover that there's a life you never imagined and see the abundance of opportunities, you begin to understand your own purpose.

God wants us to be fearless. He wants us to use our time on earth for a purpose. Successful people use their time differently. Instead of playing on social media, they spend time structuring and organizing or reading up on how to complete their next project or what to invest in.

As I look back on my past, I see that I spent a lot of my time worrying about things beyond my control. I stressed about unimportant things. I didn't understand why I was going through some of the darkest days In my life or why my time was consumed with hardship, relationship issues, childish problems, and work.

One of the turning points was battling cancer. When people ask me about it, I say it was the best thing that happened to me. Time to me is the value I put on this journey. Time is giving God a moment every day. Time is allowing God to direct my path. Time is God giving us a gift we may not deserve. God gave me grace and love. God gave me a life I couldn't understand but brought me to where I'm supposed to be.

Don't waste your time.
Use your time wisely.
Stop and smell the roses.
Never ever give up on your dreams.
Go out in the world and try to make them come true.

If your thoughts become your reality, you have a purpose. Live life to the fullest without regrets in whatever way you choose, but always know that your actions have consequences. You will have dark days, but that doesn't mean there's no light at the end of the tunnel. Live a life full of love and compassion and always stay humble, but be excited. Don't compensate for lost time but make up for it in the future. Use it wisely!

Made in the USA
Columbia, SC
08 June 2025

22b06402-8905-433a-86ed-a055b9f60a51R01